BOA
EDITIONS
LIMITED

FUEL

Poems by

Naomi Shihab Nye

BOA Editions, Ltd. ∞ Rochester, New York ∞ 1998

LC #: 97–74819
ISBN: 1–880238–63–2

05 06 07 08   9 8 7 6

Publications by BOA Editions, Ltd.—
a not-for-profit corporation under section 501 (c) (3)
of the United States Internal Revenue Code—
are made possible with the assistance of grants from
the Literature Program of the New York State Council on the Arts,
the Literature Program of the National Endowment for the Arts,
the Lannan Foundation, the Sonia Raiziss Giop Charitable Foundation,
the Eric Mathieu King Fund of The Academy of American Poets,
as well as from the Mary S. Mulligan Charitable Trust,
the County of Monroe, NY,
and from many individual supporters.

Cover Design: Daphne Poulin-Stofer
Cover Art: "Cantaloupes and Ants," by James Cobb
Author Photo: Michael Nye
Typesetting: Richard Foerster
Manufacturing: McNaughton & Gunn
BOA Logo: Mirko

BOA Editions, Ltd.
Thom Ward, Editor
David Oliveiri, Chair
A. Poulin, Jr., President & Founder (1938-1996)
260 East Avenue
Rochester, NY 14604
www.boaeditions.org

NATIONAL
ENDOWMENT
FOR THE ARTS

State of the Arts
NYSCA

With gratitude to many writers who left us in 1997,
their voices ongoing, sustaining—

F

that the mind's fire may not fail.
The *vowels of affliction*, of unhealed
not to feel it, uttered,
transformed in utterance
to song.
        Not farewell, not farewell, but faring

                                        —Denise Levertov

CONTENTS

∽

FUEL

MUCHAS GRACIAS POR TODO

This plane has landed thanks to God and his mercy.
That's what they say in Jordan when the plane sets down.

What do they say in our country? Don't stand up till we tell you.
Stay in your seats. Things may have shifted.

This river has not disappeared thanks to that one big storm
when the water was almost finished.

We used to say thanks to the springs
but the springs dried up so we changed it.

This rumor tells no truth thanks to people.
This river walk used to be better when no one came.

What about the grapes? Thanks to the grapes
we have more than one story to tell.

Thanks to a soft place in the middle of the evening.
Thanks to three secret hours before dawn.

These deer are seldom seen because of their shyness.
If you see one you count yourselves among the lucky on the earth.

Your eyes get quieter.
These deer have nothing to say to us.

Thanks to the fan, we are still breathing.
Thanks to the small toad that lives in cool mud at the base of the zinnias.

∞

BILL'S BEANS

for William Stafford

Under the leaves, they're long and curling.
I pull a perfect question mark and two lean twins,
feeling the magnetic snap of stem, the ripened weight.
At the end of a day, the earth smells thirsty.
He left his brown hat, his shovel, and his pen.
I don't know how deep bean roots go.
We could experiment.
He left the sky over Oregon and the fluent trees.
He gave us our lives that were hiding under our feet,
saying, You know what to do.
So we'll take these beans
back into the house and steam them.
We'll eat them one by one with our fingers,
the clean click and freshness.
We'll thank him forever for our breath,
and the brevity of bean.

WEDDING CAKE

Once on a plane
a woman asked me to hold her baby
and disappeared.
I figured it was safe,
our being on a plane and all.
How far could she go?

She returned one hour later,
having changed her clothes
and washed her hair.
I didn't recognize her.

By this time the baby
and I had examined
each other's necks.
We had cried a little.
I had a silver bracelet
and a watch.
Gold studs glittered
in the baby's ears.
She wore a tiny white dress
leafed with layers
like a wedding cake.

I did not want
to give her back.

The baby's curls coiled tightly
against her scalp,
another alphabet.
I read *new new new*.
My mother gets tired.
I'll chew your hand.

The baby left my skirt crumpled,
my lap aching.
Now I'm her secret guardian,
the little nub of dream
that rises slightly
but won't come clear.

As she grows,
as she feels ill at ease,
I'll bob my knee.

What will she forget?
Whom will she marry?
He'd better check with me.
I'll say once she flew
dressed like a cake
between two doilies of cloud.
She could slip the card into a pocket,
pull it out.
Already she knew the small finger
was funnier than the whole arm.

GENETICS

From my father I have inherited the ability
to stand in a field and stare.

Look, look at that gray dot by the fence.
It's his donkey. My father doesn't have
a deep interest in donkeys, more a figurative one.
To know it's out there nuzzling the ground.

That's how I feel about my life.
I like to skirt the edges. There it is in the field.
Feeding itself.

*

From my mother, an obsession about the stove
and correct spelling. The red stove, old as I am, must be
polished at all times. You don't know this about me.
I do it when you're not home.

The Magic Chef gleams in his tipped hat.
Oven shoots to 500 when you set it low.
Then fluctuates. Like a personality.

Thanks to my mother I now have an oven thermometer
but must open the oven door to check it.
Even when a cake's in there. Isn't this supposed to be
disaster for a cake?

My mother does crosswords, which I will never do.
But a word spelled wrongly anywhere
prickles my skin. Return to beginning
with pencil, black ink.
Cross you at the "a." Rearrange.
We had family discussions
about a preference for the British *grey*.

In the spelling bee I tripped on *reveille*,
a bugle call, a signal at dawn.
I have risen early
ever since.

BECAUSE OF LIBRARIES WE CAN SAY THESE THINGS

She is holding the book close to her body,
carrying it home on the cracked sidewalk,
down the tangled hill.
If a dog runs at her again, she will use the book as a shield.

She looked hard among the long lines
of books to find this one.
When they start talking about money,
when the day contains such long and hot places,
she will go inside.
An orange bed is waiting.
Story without corners.
She will have two families.
They will eat at different hours.

She is carrying a book past the fire station
and the five-and-dime.
What this town has not given her
the book will provide; a sheep,
a wilderness of new solutions.
The book has already lived through its troubles.
The book has a calm cover, a straight spine.

When the step returns to itself
as the best place for sitting,
and the old men up and down the street
are latching their clippers,

she will not be alone.
She will have a book to open
and open and open.
Her life starts here.

ELEVATOR

We jumped in, trusting
the slow swish of heavy doors,

punching 7, 9, 12.
O swoon of rising stomach! Then a sudden drop.

We took turns popping envelopes into the mail chute
& watching them whiz by from a lower floor.

Where are you? Calling down the tunnel,
sweet high ding, nobody's dinnerbell.

In stepped the lady with a fur muff,
her elegant gentleman smelling of New York.

We sobered our faces, bit the glinting arrows
while our father sorted receipts off the lobby.

Good-bye! we called to him again & again.
His desk wore a little spike.

Where are you going?
We are going!

Breathing rich perfume & dust
ground into burgundy carpet,

we glistened in the polished edge
of everything that didn't belong to us,

suitcases, humming radios,
brass locks, canisters for ash.

With nowhere to go we became
specialists in Ups & Downs.

Brother! I cried, as he rose to the penthouse without me.
Sister! He wailed, as I sank deep into the ground.

CAPE COD

The graves of Desire Nye and Patty Nye (1794)
and the two Mehitabels who lived one year each.
William and Ebenezer and Samuel Nye
and the wives and cousins and the one with no hands.
Deep, deep in the ground that is cracking.

We jog and skip the ditch.
Your red shirt, your tipped cap.
Is it strange to see your name
on so many stones? *I am not alone.*
A riddle hangs by a single corner
like a towel pinned on a line.
We forget to bring it in for days.

It barely waves, taking on
the shape of the sea.
Whose towel was it?
In the sun a pebble glitters.
A hundred thousand pebbles line the sand
where Henry David Thoreau
ate a giant clam and threw it up.
Ebenezer fell into the mouth of the whale.

Henry was sad here.
He wrote his gloomiest essay
after a shipwreck, all the ladies
floating dead into shore.
That's what you get for traveling.

But this other lady with no hands
stayed close to home sewing quilts.
How? The riddle blinks.
Tiny green triangles poked nose-to-nose.
We saw them in the house
down the road.

Can we find a silver needle
in her hem?

BEING FROM ST. LOUIS

Under the nickel-gray bridges
the rumbling trains snaked over,
and the bitter gray rain
draining toward holes in the streets,
beneath buildings with teeth for windows,
the Veiled Prophet floated past
in his strange parade. No one knew who he was.
I cracked my head on cement when the giant lion
opened his jaws to roar NO always NO
but we were going to do it anyway.

Over the scum of the fallen gray leaves
and winter's fist that held and held
till every secret tip of the tree was frozen,
beside the gray river that marked us off—
what did east or west mean if you were in the center?—
and its splintered, floating debris,
we left our smallest clothes behind.

Under the bent gray sky and its month-long frown,
the gloomy wisdom of red brick and the silver Arch
that would surely fall, we said,
standing nervously off to one side
as the last gleaming segment swung into place
on the hook of a giant crane—

  That would surely fall.

Come tumbling down.

Since those days we became people
who blink harder in sunlight,
flying into our old city
staring from the plane

It didn't fall   after all

who have become the gray rain
in a quiet place under our skins,
returning to the house still standing,
to the trees who do not see us,
to the schoolyard to pick up
one pencil-sized stick from the rich gravel.
Who carry it home as we would have done
in another life when the earth was still writing
its name on our knees.

EYE TEST

The D is desperate.
The B wants to take a vacation,
live on a billboard, be broad and brave.
The E is mad at the R for upstaging him.
The little c wants to be a big C if possible,
and the P pauses long between thoughts.

How much better to be a story, story.
Can you read me?

We have to live on this white board
together like a neighborhood.
We would rather be the tail of a cloud,
one letter becoming another,
or lost in a boy's pocket
shapeless as lint,
the same boy who squints to read us
believing we convey a secret message.
    Be his friend.
We are so tired of meaning nothing.

THE SMALL VASES FROM HEBRON

Tip their mouths open to the sky.
Turquoise, amber,
the deep green with fluted handle,
pitcher the size of two thumbs,
tiny lip and graceful waist.

Here we place the smallest flower
which could have lived invisibly
in loose soil beside the road,
sprig of succulent rosemary,
bowing mint.

They grow deeper in the center of the table.

Here we entrust the small life,
thread, fragment, breath.
And it bends. It waits all day.
As the bread cools and the children
open their gray copybooks
to shape the letter that looks like
a chimney rising out of a house.

And what do the headlines say?

Nothing of the smaller petal
perfectly arranged inside the larger petal
or the way tinted glass filters light.
Men and boys, praying when they died,
fall out of their skins.
The whole alphabet of living,
heads and tails of words,
sentences, the way they said,
"Ya'Allah!" when astonished,
or "ya'ani" for "I mean"—
a crushed glass under the feet

still shines.
But the child of Hebron sleeps
with the thud of her brothers falling
and the long sorrow of the color red.

DARLING

1.

I break this toast for the ghost of bread in Lebanon.
The split stone, the toppled doorway.

Someone's kettle has been crushed.
Someone's sister has a gash above her right eye.

And now our tea has trouble being sweet.
A strawberry softens, turns musty,

overnight each apple grows a bruise.
I tie both shoes on Lebanon's feet.

All day the sky in Texas that has seen no rain since June
is raining Lebanese mountains, Lebanese trees.

What if the air grew damp with the names of mothers?
The clear-belled voices of first graders

pinned to the map of Lebanon like a shield?
When I visited the camp of the opposition

near the lonely Golan, looking northward toward
Syria and Lebanon, a vine was springing pinkly from a tin can

and a woman with generous hips like my mother's
said, "Follow me."

2.

Someone was there. Someone not there now
was standing. In the wrong place
with a small moon-shaped scar on his cheek
and a boy by the hand.

Who had just drunk water, sharing the glass.
Not thinking about it deeply
though they might have, had they known.
Someone grown and someone not-grown.
Who imagined they had different amounts of time left.
This guessing-game ends with our hands in the air,
becoming air.
One who was there is not there, for no reason.
Two who were there.

It was almost too big to see.

3.

Our friend from Turkey says language is so delicate
he likens it to a darling.

We will take this word in our arms:
It will be small and breathing.
We will not wish to scare it.
Pressing lips to the edge of each syllable.
Nothing else will save us now.
The word "together" wants to live in every house.

ONE BOY TOLD ME

Music lives inside my legs.
It's coming out when I talk.

I'm going to send my valentines
to people you don't even know.

Oatmeal cookies make my throat gallop.

Grown-ups keep their feet on the ground
when they swing. I hate that.

Look at those 2 o's with a smash in the middle—
that spells good-bye.

Don't ever say "purpose" again,
let's throw the word out.

Don't talk big to me.
I'm carrying my box of faces.
If I want to change faces I will.

Yesterday faded
but tomorrow's in BOLDFACE.

When I grow up my old names
will live in the house
where we live now.
I'll come and visit them.

Only one of my eyes is tired.
The other eye and my body aren't.

Is it true all metal was liquid first?
Does that mean if we bought our car earlier
they could have served it
in a cup?

There's a stopper in my arm
that's not going to let me grow any bigger.
I'll be like this always, small.

And I will be deep water too.
Wait. Just wait. How deep is the river?
Would it cover the tallest man with his hands in the air?

Your head is a souvenir.

When you were in New York I could see you
in real life walking in my mind.

I'll invite a bee to live in your shoe.
What if you found your shoe
full of honey?

What if the clock said 6:92
instead of 6:30? Would you be scared?

My tongue is the car wash
for the spoon.

Can noodles swim?

My toes are dictionaries.
Do you need any words?

From now on I'll only drink white milk
on January 26.

What does minus mean?
I never want to minus you.

Just think—no one has ever seen
inside this peanut before!

It is hard being a person.

I do and don't love you—
isn't that happiness?

BOY AND MOM AT THE NUTCRACKER BALLET

There's no talking in this movie.

> It's not a movie! Just watch the dancers.
> They tell the story through their dancing.

Why is the nutcracker mean?

> I think because the little boy broke him.

Did the little boy mean to?

> Probably not.

Why did the nutcracker stab his sword through the mouse king?
I liked the mouse king.

> So did I. I don't know. I wish that part wasn't in it.

You can see that girl's underpants.

> No, not underpants. It's a costume called a "tutu"—same word
> as "grandmother" in Hawaiian.

Are those real gems on their costumes?
Do they get to keep them?
Is that really snow coming down?

> No, it can't be, it would melt and their feet get wet.

I think it's white paper.

> Aren't they beautiful?

They are very beautiful. But what do the dancers do when we can't see them, when they're off the stage and they're not dancing?
Do you have any more pistachios in your purse?

PASSING IT ON

Our son's shirts attend kindergarten
for the third time.
They are still learning how to share.

*

To wear my friend's lace camisole
I had to become a new person.

Since I was plenty tired of myself,
it was a pleasure.

*

Closets bulging
with gingham castoffs,
calico and rickrack denim,
my mother begs, "Enough."

But when I gave
her dotted swiss curtains
to the Salvation Army,
she was inconsolable.
One can't be too careful.

*

I'm in my linen period now.
That casual crumple,
that wrinkled weight,
sustains.

*

My father won't enter
a secondhand store.
He pitched his extra pants into the Atlantic
when he started his new life.

Under Ellis Island
whole wardrobes may be mingling
with seaweed,
buckling and bobbing with fish.

I wish for once to be dressed
in something sleek and thin
as original skin.

ALWAYS BRING A PENCIL

There will not be a test.
It does not have to be
a Number 2 pencil.

But there will be certain things—
the quiet flush of waves,
ripe scent of fish,
smooth ripple of the wind's second name—
that prefer to be written about
in pencil.

It gives them more room
to move around.

YOUR NAME ENGRAVED ON A GRAIN OF RICE

Blazing pink shirts spill into streets, garden green, full-throated
fluorescent, fiesta red. Humdrum the dim subtleties! The mothers haul

parasols for sun toward Ferris wheels which may or may not have that last pin
properly placed. Who cares, these days? You could die just eating.

They drag small stools for sitting at parades and toddling boys who kick
the giant Coke cups pitched onto curbs, toeing the sweet and sticky trails.

Thirsty places inside their mouths grow and grow. Soon they too would spend
extra for what they usually pour from the big bottle in front of TV.

City Hall shrinks in a cluttered grid of Tilt-a-Whirls and Rocket Rides.
Now our local headliners may watch their constituents flip upside down

for fun. How much have they done to lose our faith? See them reach their
people here, propellers of hair spinning out. See the people thread

the crowd to smash a bottle with a ball. All they need
is a break in schedule to sizzle again. Give them kings, confetti,

cascarón eggs cracked over their heads. Dribble of itchy bits down the back
of the shirt, who cares, insurance, who cares, brown spots on the back of the

hand? In this land of glistening ballgowns and floats of flashing girls,
everything shifts. Even if her waving hand is gone

in two minutes. They trade in lonely houses for the crowd,
beer-scented blaring, bras without shirts,

the sloping, sweltering flesh. They mesh. They lose their quarters. They
guffaw. They ought to do what that booth says, put their name on the littlest

grain of rice like magic, but what about Fernando, Dagoberto,
Henrietta, Marielena? Aren't they too long? What about Octavio

Hernandez-Salvatierra and his 20 uncles and their 77 hopes? What about the year we planned to trick everything gloomy like a bad yard

with sudden roses turning nice or something that swells and stays swelled, bubbling and softening, changing its life?

SAN ANTONIO MI SANGRE: FROM THE HARD SEASON

*We have faith that God . . . is the owner of water and the
one who could really help us with this.*

—Rev. Rodolfo Ruiz, during prayers for the drought

The 2 A.M. whistle of the long train
stretches out the thread between days,

pins it in a crack between its teeth and pulls
so the people in white beds by the flour mill

become the wheat
unground in the sacks

and the old fish with one whisker
flips over in the river grown too thin.

We need the rain, the iron bar of the track,
the backside of heat. Perfect V-ripple eleven ducklings
cast swimming toward the shore for bread.

As the boys who will not lift their heads
to look anyone in the eye mark the name of their pack

on the bridge with the stink of squared-off letters,
Señora Esquivel who lives alone

remembers her underwear draped on the line.
It will not rain tonight, has not rained in 90 nights.

Cantaloupe cracks on the inside,
jagged fissures in orange flesh.

When the cat blinks to see the sneaky possum
licking his water dish dry,

he thinks, and thinks, Tomorrow I'll get him.
Then sleeps. Inside the small breeze

lifting the fringe of the train's held tone
Hondo, Sabinal, Uvalde, Del Rio, and far off,

glittering as Oz, El Paso rising
from its corner, holding the giant state in place

as a dozing conductor grips his swatch of tickets firmly
in a car streaking the thirsty land.

WIND AND THE SLEEPING BREATH OF MEN

From far away
from the faraway inside each life
the island a minor disruption

all night shearing off corners
scattering the palm's dried wings
as wind claims the whole sky

telling the wild story
you who arranged your desks
papers in the right-
and left-hand corners
bow down

*

All day the men took air into their bodies
and traded it back again

the men and women took air into their bodies
growing great parachutes over their heads

and the children gulping whole lungfuls
saying they weren't hungry
breathed the same air
as an old neighbor dutifully sweeping his leaves
into a packet
tied with rope

at the top of the mountain
we were breathing air that used to drift
around the bottom of the mountain

resting in a forest
breathing the hush and rustle of bamboo

I wanted to trade something larger
than what I had taken

*

Nothing worse for the person
who can't sleep
than to lie beside
heavy sleepers

first you envy
then worry about them
each hair in their nostrils
growing more delicate

each inhalation a small balcony
from which you wave good-bye
to your lives passing
in the thousand streets
beyond reach

WHAT'S HERE

Idaho potatoes have made it to Honolulu.
Scores of automobiles, legions of shirts,
rice steamers, bicycles,
as well as unlikely accessories—
bowling pin salt- and pepper-shakers,
glittering eye shadow,
chocolate-covered cherries,
washed up on these shores.
Outlandish as it seems, all these
preceded us.

The leaves of Eucalyptus robusta
try not to notice it.
Wild purple orchid,
sleek bark of koa,
stand clear. What's here
may or may not belong here.
I press my extra eyes
into the mist over the valley,
forgetting my small book of stamps
and the ten thousand travelers
eating breakfast,
guarding the word *invisible*,
sweet breath of every tree.
I ride the waves of vowels, saying
in my own flat language,
I'll go soon. And, don't remember me.

WAIKIKI

On the famous beach in Honolulu a small Japanese girl cried and cried and cried. She stood stiff-legged, poking her feet into the sand. Her parents kneeled, whispered, cajoled. Then they tried walking away. They had a baby in their arms. They strolled surprisingly far down the beach, but never took their eyes off her. She raised the volume on her crying, staring straight out to sea. Her pink bathing suit, its ruffled rump. Our eyes followed the silver planes rising off the runway. I loved every plane I was not on. I loved the wailing girl who saw no one else on that beach but herself, whose throat worked hard to find the biggest, saddest sound. After her parents gave up and dragged her still screaming down the beach, we went and sat by the poked-in place her feet had made and funneled up the billion particles into a mound.

ONGOING

The shape of talk would sag
but the birds be brighter than ever

O I needed the birds worse & worse as I got older
as if some crack had opened in the human scheme of things
& only birds with their sharp morning notes
had the sense for any new day

The people went round & round
in the old arenas
dragging their sacks
of troubles & stones & jaggedy love
I could not help them
I was one of them
the people pitched advice
in its flat hat back & forth
across the table

But the birds so far above us
hardly complete sentences
just fragments & dashes
the birds who had seen the towns
grow up & topple
who caught the changing wind
before anyone on the ground did
who left for Mexico when we were not
paying attention
what could they tell us
about lives in heavy bodies

what could they tell us
about being
caught?

&

BOY'S SLEEP

All day a boy plunges his hands into his pockets.
Tickets, tape, crystallized stones, a two-dollar bill.

He will not wear pants without pockets.
It is a point of honor.

He sleeps as deeply as the crackle of the burning log,
the breath of the far-flung sea.

Where are you, world? Don't do anything
while I'm not paying attention.

GLINT - Prose poem

My grandmother mentioned only once how the piano teacher she had as a girl leaned over her too closely at the keys. His damp lips grazed her cheek or maybe they touched her mouth for a minute. My grandmother never felt comfortable with the piano after that. I think a little more music could have helped her life. I played her piano sometimes. Dust rose in little clouds from the cracks between the keys. A few keys had lost their voices. My grandmother told me some things but not enough. We had a sweetness between us. What happened to the piano teacher? His lips parting ever so slightly over middle C, eyes pinned to the ripe notes on the sheet . . . could he help it what they reminded him of? Here I am trying to gather her lost kisses from the air. They're drifting just outside the tune.

EARLY RISER

The face of the clock at 4 A.M.
doesn't have many friends.
Its wishes are thin and dark,
to stay humble, close to the floor.

Without it I am a crumb of talk
stuck to a plate.
The day unfolds its sad sack of chores,
the broom loses two more hairs.

Without it I am the letter carrier
who never receives
any mail herself.

FUNDAMENTALISM

Because the eye has a short shadow or
it is hard to see over heads in the crowd?

If everyone else seems smarter
but you need your own secret?

If mystery was never your friend?

If one way could satisfy
the infinite heart of the heavens?

If you liked the king on his golden throne
more than the villagers carrying baskets of lemons?

If you wanted to be sure
his guards would admit you to the party?

       The boy with the broken pencil
       scrapes his little knife against the lead
       turning and turning it as a point
       emerges from the wood again

       If he would believe his life is like that
       he would not follow his father into war

DUCKS

We thought of ourselves as people of culture.
How long will it be till others see us that way again?
Iraqi friend

In her first home each book had a light around it.
The voices of distant countries
floated in through open windows,
entering her soup and her mirror.
They slept with her in the same thick bed.

Someday she would go there.
Her voice, among all those voices.
In Iraq a book never had one owner—it had ten.
Lucky books, to be held often
and gently, by so many hands.

Later in American libraries she felt sad
for books no one ever checked out.

She lived in a country house beside a pond
and kept ducks, two male, one female.
She worried over the difficult relations
of triangles. One of the ducks
often seemed depressed.
But not the same one.

During the war between her two countries
she watched the ducks more than usual.
She stayed quiet with the ducks.
Some days they huddled among reeds
or floated together.

She could not call her family in Basra
which had grown farther away than ever
nor could they call her. For nearly a year

she would not know who was alive,
who was dead.

The ducks were building a nest.

NEW YEAR

Over our heads the words hung down
with giant sparkling margins.
I was try-trying again
every day of my life.
That's why I've been followed
by stacks of blank notebooks, why
any calendar page with nothing written on it
strikes me full of ravenous joy.

When a year changes,
the little stuffed man
pitches into the flames,
his paper-bag body fattened by
ragged lists, crumpled mail.
Between 8 P.M. when I scrawl
the vanishing year on his chest
and midnight, we fall in love.

His rueful grin, his crooked hat!

He burns fast in the backyard pit.
Then a deep quiet plucked by firecrackers
under a weirdly lit city sky.

No plans come to mind.
I just stand there with my hands out
in smoke while something else
wonderful dies.

MY FRIEND'S DIVORCE

I want her
to dig up
every plant
in her garden
the pansies
the pentas
roses
ranunculus
thyme and lilies
the thing nobody knows
the name of
unwind the morning glories
from the wire windows
of the fence
take the blooming
and the almost-blooming
and the dormant
especially the dormant
and then
and then
plant them in her new yard
on the other side
of town
and see how
they breathe

VISIT

Welcome to Abu Dhabi,
the Minister of Culture said.
You may hold my falcon as we visit.
He slipped a leather band around my arm
and urged the bird to step on board.
It wore a shapely leather hood,
Or otherwise, the host described,
the bird might pluck your very eyes.
My very eyes were blinking hard
behind the glasses that they wore.
The falcon's claws, so hooked and huge,
gripped firmly on the leather band.
I had to hold my arm out high.
My hand went numb. The heavens shone
a giant gold beyond our room.
I had no memory why I'd come
to see this man.
A falcon dives, and rips, and kills!
I think he likes you though.
It was the most I could have hoped for then.
We mentioned art.
We drank some tea.
He offered to remove the hood.
I said the bird looked very good just wearing it.
Alright by me.

THE PALESTINIANS HAVE GIVEN UP PARTIES

Once singing would rise
in sweet sirens over the hills
and even if you were working
with your trees or books
or cooking something simple
for your own family,
you washed your hands,
combed water through your hair.

Mountains of rice, shiny shoes,
a hurricane of dancing.
Children wearing little suitcoats
and velvet dresses fell asleep in circles
after eating 47 Jordan almonds.

Who's getting married? Who's come home
from the far place over the seas?

Sometimes you didn't even know.
You ate all that food without knowing.
Kissed both cheeks of anybody who passed,
slapping the drum, reddening your palm.
Later you were full, rich,
with a party in your skin.

Where does fighting
come into this story?

Fighting got lost from somewhere else.
It is not what we like: to eat, to drink, *to fight.*

Now when the students gather quietly
inside their own classroom
to celebrate the last day of school,
the door to the building

gets blasted off.
Empty chairs where laughter used to sit.
Laughter lived here
jingling its pocket of thin coins
and now it is hiding.

It will not come to the door dressed as a soapseller,
a peddler of matches, the old Italian
from the factory in Nablus
with his magic sack of sticks.

They have told us we are not here
when we were always here.
Their eraser does not work.

See the hand-tinted photos of young men:
too perfect, too still.
The bombs break everyone's
sentences in half.
Who made them? Do you know anyone
who makes them? The ancient taxi driver
shakes his head back and forth
from Jerusalem to Jericho.
They will not see, he says slowly,
the story behind the story,
they are always looking for the story after the story
which means they will never understand the story.

Which means it will go on and on.

How can we stand it if it goes on and on?
It is too long already.
No one even gets a small bent postcard
from the far place over the seas anymore.

No one hears the soldiers come at night
to pluck the olive tree from its cool sleep.

Ripping up roots. This is not a headline
in your country or mine.
No one hears the tiny sobbing
of the velvet in the drawer.

HALF-AND-HALF

You can't be, says a Palestinian Christian
on the first feast day after Ramadan.
So, half-and-half and half-and-half.
He sells glass. He knows about broken bits,
chips. If you love Jesus you can't love
anyone else. Says he.

At his stall of blue pitchers on the Via Dolorosa,
he's sweeping. The rubbed stones
feel holy. Dusting of powdered sugar
across faces of date-stuffed *mamool*.

This morning we lit the slim white candles
which bend over at the waist by noon.
For once the priests weren't fighting
in the church for the best spots to stand.
As a boy, my father listened to them fight.
This is partly why he prays in no language
but his own. Why I press my lips
to every exception.

A woman opens a window—here and here and here—
placing a vase of blue flowers
on an orange cloth. I follow her.
She is making a soup from what she had left
in the bowl, the shriveled garlic and bent bean.
She is leaving nothing out.

BUTTER BOX

*To close: Fold in small end flaps. Insert Flap A
into Flap B as shown.*

There is a picture to help us.
Also an announcement: *Carton has been opened.*
In case we are stumbling through an afternoon,
have lost our way, or plate and knife confound us.

Once a plastic bag intoned: *There should be a suggestion
of firmness in the cooked macaroni.* Not entirely firm,
not utterly anything, just a *suggestion.*

But I don't want to close the butter box
with the butter in it. Place a single brick
in the pink dish, extra three

stacked in waiting, box discarded.
See how much help we didn't need?

∞

SMOKE

The new slash of road curves up beside five sleeping smokestacks.
Four stand together, one apart—the lucky or the lonely one, depending.

I'm driving you to school with your blue pants and box of lunch.
I'm combing your hair with my eyes.

They've built fancy houses around a giant pit. What do people see in it?
The smokestacks were smoking when I was in college, when my father

drove me down the old road on the other side.
Was it neat? We both know smoke isn't neat but I guess

what you mean. Was it black or white? I can't recall.
So much has poured out the top of my head.

I knew the lady who owned the smokestacks, her peacock
bit my hand. We take turns imagining what happens next,

if they stand or fall, whether the wrecked warehouse
with arches will be spared, or the fog lift, or the sun.

Today a small red light glitters at the throat of the lucky one.
You call it a good sign. At school your friends wear puffy coats

bright as parrots. You fly into your teacher's arms.
I could even hug a dull-looking father in his necktie

as we roll out of the lot into our daily lives. When I pass
the smokestacks again, their firm ladders

and proud ALAMO lettering up the sides, I'm fiddling
with the radio dial, swinging into a lane of cars.

Now the gloom of distant news washes over worse than grit
and we can't clean it, fix it, or make good sense.

Still we hold our mouths wide open, and the birds,
the sky, the trees, and the river

fly into us as if anything could heal. Somewhere deep,
these years must be churning the way cement does

inside a truck. The cement those smokestacks helped to make—
it became sidewalks all over this city. It became

buildings and tunnels and walls. We don't think of it gleaming.
Even the highway I drive on.

ALONE

He grows used to the sound of the floor
Not yet   Not yet   each evening
right before the news comes on.

Then the killing and the stabbing
and the beating and the crashing.
Turn it off. There's a smudge on the wall,
a Jesus with a blazing heart.

His coffee cup waits
upside down on its plate.
The shape of dinner tastes upside down.
He eats whatever the nurse-lady left him,
the hamburger in its three-day shirt.
Sometimes he doesn't know the name
of what he eats.

He hauls his body to the porch,
sinks his eyes into the weeds.
A hose curls in the lilies.
If he could reach it,
make it down
those three crooked steps . . .

When his wife died he was very quiet
for one day. Then he smiled
and smiled with his two teeth
for the bad time they had
that was over.

His tongue could sound *Soledad* or *Solamente*
for his bones and his blood and his few good hairs.

When the drop of water on the white sink
meets the next drop and they are joining,
he thinks of other ways to spend this life
that he didn't do. He would like to meet them.

ALPHABET

One by one
the old people
of our neighborhood
are going up
into the air

their yards
still wear
small white narcissus
sweetening winter

their stones
glisten
under the sun
but one by one
we are losing
their housecoats
their formal phrasings
their cupcakes

When I string their names
on the long cord

when I think how
there is almost no one left
who remembers
what stood in that
brushy spot
ninety years ago

when I pass their yards
and the bare peach tree
bends a little

when I see their rusted chairs

sitting in the same spots

what will be forgotten
falls over me
like the sky
over our whole neighborhood

or the time my plane
circled high above our street
the roof of our house
dotting the tiniest
"i"

FEATHER

She's walking up the street from Sanitary Tortilla
with her pink mesh shopping bag.
Mrs. Esquivel of the waving plants,
front porch lined with leaves.
In softer light she dances with sheets.

She came here from the old days.
Slipped out of the old days like a feather.
Floated here with her aluminum pot lids
and blue enamel spoons tied to her wings.
Fanning the heat away with an apron,
ruffled rickrack edge.
She believed in the screen door,
its tiny holes letting in breeze.
She preceded thieves and reasons for locking.
She held on to all her paper fans.

Her *¿Como estas?* has a heart in it.
If I said *No good,* she would listen.

*

*Honey how's the little one? I see him come out
on the porch in his red shirt,
pick up the hose, shoot it straight
in the air at the bananas.
You got any ripe yet?
I walk over to see the President of the United States
at the Alamo and he don't look like much.
He stand up high on a little stage and look down
into our faces. He got that tight look
like the curly-tail dog sit in the middle
of the street every night when the lamps
go on. Why you think it do that?
I say, Hey! Hey you! Trucks!*

68

*And it turn its head, look at me
so up and down like I'm the one
who crazy.*

*

Sometimes the grass grows so tall
in the vacant lot beside her house.
Fancy pink vines tie knots
around the heads of weeds.
She swims through the field at sundown,
calling out to hens, cats, whoever
might be lost in there,
Hey! Hey you! It's time to come home!

And the people drifting slowly past
in the slim envelope of light
answer softly, *Here I am.*

69

HIDDEN

If you place a fern
under a stone
the next day it will be
nearly invisible
as if the stone has
swallowed it.

If you tuck the name of a loved one
under your tongue too long
without speaking it
it becomes blood
sigh
the little sucked-in breath of air
hiding everywhere
beneath your words.

No one sees
the fuel that feeds you.

WAITING TO CROSS

One man closes his hand.
He will not show us
the silver buckle
he uncovered in his garden.

One man reads houses.
They make sense to him,
grammar of lights in windows.
He looks for a story to be part of.

One man has no friends.
His mother is shrinking
at a table with one chair.
She dreams a mouse
with her son's small head.

One man feels right.
The others must be wrong.
And the world? It does not touch him.

One man stares hard
at the other men's profiles
against the sky.
He knows he is one of five men
standing on a corner.

ESTATE SALE

A crowd of strangers flies over your life
picking out landmarks—stainless steel
cake pan, jello mold, pastel box of
thank you notes. Someone's even put
a 25-cent price tag on the coffin
of Kleenex in the bathroom.

I'm a prowler, unable to smile back
at the bouyant women hired to coordinate
this last event.

Beside the dismantled bedframe,
a telephone with scrawled number of
SON DAVID EVANS taped to the side.

You intended it to be read by someone else.
I hope he came by often including you
in his regular weeks, not just his holidays.

Your angels with lace collars.
Christmas cookie plate
and rattled tea towels.

How big we are, the living.

We stomp between your flexible curtain road
and the dictionary with a chunk torn out.

I'm caught in the kitchen with a sadness
flat as the icebox door.
Considering reductions: your horizon,
your hope. Antique wooden wardrobes
stuffed into three tight rooms.

Carrying the stack of blank typing paper
and the Scrabble game with the Santa sticker
circa 1950.
Now we're stuck together.

Wooden letters click in our hands.
We make ABLE, ADEPT.
Someone's JIG turns into JIGSAW.

Someone's HUNCH remains just that,
though we keep flying over it from different angles,
trying to make it larger,
trying to give it feet or hands or another ground
to stand on.

LOST

notices   flutter

      from   telephone   poles

          until   they   fade

OUR SWEET TABBY   AFRAID OF EVERYTHING

BIG GRAY CAT   HE IS OUR ONLY CHILD

SIBERIAN HUSKY   NEEDS HIS MEDICINE

FEMALE SCHNAUZER   WE ARE SICK WITH WORRY

all night I imagine their feet
tapping up the sidewalk
under the blooming crepe myrtle
and the swoon of jasmine
into the secret hedges
into the dark cool caves
of the banana-palm grove
and we cannot catch them
or know what they are thinking
when they go so far from home

OUR BELOVED TURTLE   RED DOT ON FOREHEAD
VEGETARIAN   NAME OF KALI

please   please   please

      if you see them

call me   call me   call me

PUFF

Somehow our grandfather's old smoking cabinet
which held playing cards and pipes
has ended up in my brother's guest bedroom
a thousand miles from Union Boulevard
where men dragged bundled laundry
in heavy carts down the street before dawn.

I feel startled each time I see it, expecting
the crisp dachshund who lived inside
and puffed smoke rings, doughnuts rising
from his tiny white cigarette—how did he get away?
Our grandfather's only toy.
They all ran, the gingham aprons and funnels,
the clock with an honest face.

Now we weigh an hour for a space
belonging to us.
Once it all belonged to us.
Our grandfather's long chair, the slope
of his arm resting as he slept.
He had German words inside his tongue.
He lit a cigarette for the dog with a squat body
and leaned back.

The rings said Zero Zero Zero
rising into the shades
drawn shut in the daytime.
Zero against tears.
Zero against assorted sandwich cookies
in frilled cups.
Zero against the broom and the saltshaker
and the Dutch cleanser aching in the cracks of the tiles.

We went home to a street called Harvey
wanting the thing which could not happen.

Everyone to get along.
The dog thought it could happen.
Our grandfather who lit the match
carried a hat in his hands.
Where is his bed? His lamp?

*

I am confident the street called Harvey
lives in the zippered compartment of my purse.
It is mine forever. No one could steal it.
Giving me everything I go by,
my dictionary for *pine* and *blame* and *snow*.

On another street called Salah Eddin, a shopkeeper
called out, *Your father was the most handsome man
in Jerusalem when he left!*
Tears for the men and women
who leave the places that know them.
For the streets we cannot fix
and the gray school copybooks,
weeks plotted neatly in Arabic
as if days were really square.

We marched from Tuesday to Wednesday cleanly.
Streets were the blood of our bodies;
and just as you could say veins or arteries
carried red or blue depending on whether
they were coming or going, so we each traveled
our streets coming and going at exactly the same moment—
cells, scraps, puffs of living smoke.

SNOW

Once with my scarf knotted over my mouth
I lumbered into a storm of snow up the long hill
and did not know where I was going except to the top of it.
In those days we went out like that.
Even children went out like that.
Someone was crying hard at home again,
raging blizzard of sobs.

I dragged the sled by its rope,
which we normally did not do
when snow was coming down so hard,
pulling my brother whom I called by our secret name
as if we could be other people under the skin.
The snow bit into my face, prickling the rim
of the head where the hair starts coming out.
And it was a big one. It would come down and down
for days. People would dig their cars out like potatoes.

How are you doing back there? I shouted,
and he said *Fine, I'm doing fine,*
in the sunniest voice he could muster
and I think I should love him more today
for having used it.

At the top we turned and he slid down,
steering himself with the rope gripped in
his mittened hands. I stumbled behind
sinking deeply, shouting *Ho! Look at him go!*
as if we were having a good time.
Alone on the hill. That was the deepest
I ever went into snow. Now I think of it
when I stare at paper or into silences
between human beings. The drifting
accumulation. A father goes months
without speaking to his son.

How there can be a place
so cold any movement saves you.

Ho! You bang your hands together,
stomp your feet. *The father could die!*
The son! Before the weather changes.

STEPS

A man letters the sign for his grocery in Arabic and English.
Paint dries more quickly in English.
The thick swoops and curls of Arabic letters stay moist
and glistening till tomorrow when the children show up
jingling their dimes.

They have learned the currency of the New World,
carrying wishes for gum and candies shaped like fish.
They float through the streets, diving deep to the bottom,
nosing rich layers of crusted shell.

One of these children will tell a story that keeps her people
alive. We don't know yet which one she is.
Girl in the red sweater dangling a book bag,
sister with eyes pinned to the barrel of pumpkin seeds.
They are lettering the sidewalk with their steps.

They are separate and together and a little bit late.
Carrying a creased note, "Don't forget."
Who wrote it? They've already forgotten.
A purple fish sticks to the back of the throat.
Their long laughs are boats they will ride and ride,
making the shadows that cross each other's smiles.

BOOKS WE HAVEN'T TOUCHED IN YEARS

The person who wrote YES!
in margins
disappeared.

Someone else
tempers her enthusiasms,
makes a small "v"
on its side
for lines
worth returning to.

A farmer
stares deeply
at a winter field,
envisioning
rich rows of corn.

In the mild tone
of farmers, says
Well, good luck.

What happens to us?

He doesn't dance
beside the road.

THE RIDER

A boy told me
if he roller-skated fast enough
his loneliness couldn't catch up to him,

the best reason I ever heard
for trying to be a champion.

What I wonder tonight
pedaling hard down King William Street
is if it translates to bicycles.

A victory! To leave your loneliness
panting behind you on some street corner
while you float free into a cloud of sudden azaleas,
pink petals that have never felt loneliness,
no matter how slowly they fell.

SOLVE THEIR PROBLEMS

On the horizon, their problems
loom as long as burial mounds . . .
if we rise early enough
we can visit their problems.

Low-hanging fog.
Planes held on the runway an extra hour.
We didn't get our ginger ales till Cleveland.
Expecting some light chop, the pilot said.
Chop, now there's a word.

Their problems sound arrangeable,
building blocks in a mesh bag
strung from the doorknob.
When I hear their problems I know
what the next sentence will be.

This is how they could solve them.
This is what they could do.
Hum from the lowest place in the body.
Take the problems off like a shirt.

Will they listen?
Of course not.
Without their problems they would be too lonely.
A crisis pitch is, at least, a pitch.

If they did not have extra sofas where would they sit?
A walk without any scenery?

Easy to stand back from anybody else's problems.
My own, now there's a different feather
sticking straight up out of the wing.
I need it to fly.

☉☉

MESSENGER

Someone has been painting
NOTHING IS IMPOSSIBLE
across the backs of bus benches,
blotting out the advertisements beneath
with green so the strong silver letters
appear clearly at corners,
in front of taco stands
and hardware stores.

Whoever did this
must have done it in the dark,
clanging paint cans block to block
or a couple of sprays—
they must have really
wanted to do it.

Among the many distasteful graffiti on earth
this line seems somehow honorable.
It wants to help us.
It could belong to anyone,
Latinas, Arabs, Jews,
priests, glue sniffers.
Mostly I wonder about
what happened or didn't happen
in the painter's life
to give her this line.
I don't wonder about the person
who painted HIV under the STOPs
on the stop signs in the same way.

NOTHING IS IMPOSSIBLE

Did some miracle startle
the painter into action
or is she waiting and hoping?

Does she ride the bus with her face
pressed to the window looking
for her own message?

Daily the long wind brushes YES
through the trees.

LIVING AT THE AIRPORT

Because they lived near a major airport,
their children were always flying over their heads.

Assimilating into cloud till specks of ground life
became smaller even than lives together remembered:

the floor furnace they leapt over for whole winters,
its gaping hot breath. How far they had come from

the clumsy navy stroller in the hall with its bum wheel and brakes.
The mother used to cry, pushing that thing.

Sometimes now the father went to the airport just to see
people saying good-bye and hello. Especially the good-bye gave him relief.

Before boarding, families looked so awkward together.
Repeating, *Now you be good, hear? Give a call if you can.*

They seemed almost desperate
to get away.

Since so many suitcases had their own wheels now,
he wondered, had the old rooted suitcases gone to live in attics

stuffed with unseasonable clothes, or junkyards with disappeared cars,
and what staple of their lives might have wheels next, not to mention

wings?

STRING

At certain hours we may rest assured that nearly everyone inside
our own time zone or every adjacent time zone lies asleep and then
we may begin to speak to them through the waves and folds of their dreaming
then we may urge them on   beg them not to forget
though so many days have driven in between us and original hopes
as a boy stands back from his earlier self mocking it
and the light of fireflies blinking against an old fence has become
as sad as it is lovely because so many hands are gone by now
it is not that we wanted the light to be caught   but reached for
that was it

Tonight it is possible to pull the long string and feel someone moving far away
to touch the fingers of one hand to the fingers of the other hand
to tug the bride and widow by the same thread   to be linked to every mother
every father's father   even the man in the necktie in Washington
who kept repeating *You went the wrong way, you went the wrong way*
with such animation he might have been talking about his own life

My friend took my son for his first ride on a bicycle's back fender
He said *Are you sure it is okay to do this?—We have been doing it forever*
I loped behind thinking how much has been denied him for living in a city
in the 1990s but this was a town   the dreamy grass   slow spoke
clipped hedges

Just then a light clicked on inside tall windows   draped tablecloth
pitcher of flowers   lace of evening spinning its intricate spell
inside our blood and what we smelled was earth and rain sunken into it
run-on sentence of the pavement   punctuation of night and day
giving us something to go by   a knot in the thread
although we did not live in that house

FUEL

Even at this late date, sometimes I have to look up
the word "receive." I received his deep
and interested gaze.

A bean plant flourishes under the rain of sweet words.
Tell what you think—I'm listening.

The story ruffled its twenty leaves.

*

Once my teacher set me on a high stool
for laughing. She thought the eyes
of my classmates would whittle me to size.
But they said otherwise.

We'd laugh too if we knew how.

I pinned my gaze out the window
on a ripe line of sky.

That's where I was going.

∞

COMING SOON

Today reminded me of Christmas—bright and utterly lonely.
Coleman Barks

I placed one toe
in the river of gloom.
On the streets of the cold city
a man with two raw gashes at his temple
fingered them gently.
Middle-aged sisters selling old plates and postcards
Three Floors of Bargains *** *Step Right In !*
stared glumly at a large clock.
December was just beginning.
One touched up her lipstick.
She could see herself between the 6 and 7.
Sunday-school children ate cookies
shaped like trees.
A waiter draped garlands of crumpled greenery
above the door of his restaurant,
adjusting the velvet bow.
A toothless woman wearing plastic bags
asked for the hour, which I gave her
too enthusiastically.

Here they came again.
Rolls of wrapping paper.
Red letters of ads.
I wasn't hungry
for the countdown.
Cluttered days
so sharp they cut.
What about our people
on the giant list of loves?
What would we give them
this time around?
The days say we will

look and look and look.
I plunged my foot
into the river of gloom,
it said it did not need me.

PANCAKES WITH SANTA

Santa has a bad memory.

Santa forgets your name
the minute he talks
to the next person.

Santa calls you by a baby's name
and doesn't even know.
Ho! Ho! Ho!
Should you tell Santa?
Already he thought you were a girl
though you just had a haircut
last week.
How can he remember
all those wishes?
How will Santa ever find
our house?

The world has turned to
red sweaters, jingles,
freezing rain.

Santa says he's on a diet,
that's why he's not eating pancakes
with the rest of us.
Mrs. Claus told him to
lose some weight.

Santa keeps drifting back
for more chatting.
He sits down at our table.

What else can we say to Santa?
Santa says *ain't*.

ALASKA

The phone rang in the middle of the Fairbanks night and was always a wrong number for the Klondike Lounge. *Not here*, I'd say sleepily. *Different place. We're a bunch of people rolled up in quilts.* Then I'd lie awake wondering, But how is it over there at the Klondike? The stocky building nestled between parking lots a few blocks from our apartment like some Yukon explorer's good dream of smoky windows and chow. Surely the comforting click of pool balls, the scent of old grease, flannel, and steam. Back home in Texas we got wrong numbers for the local cable TV company. People were convinced I was a secretary who didn't want to talk to them. They'd call four times in a row. *Sir*, I eventually told a determined gentleman, *We've been monitoring your viewing and are sorry to report you watch entirely too much television. You are currently ineligible for cable services. Try reading a book or something.* He didn't call back. For the Klondike Lounge I finally mumbled, *Come on over, the beer is on us.*

SO THERE

Because I would not let one four-year-old son
eat frosted mini-wheat cereal
fifteen minutes before dinner
he wrote a giant note
and held it up
while I talked on the phone

LOVE HAS FAILED

then he wrote the word LOVE
on a paper
stapled it twenty times
and said

I STAPLE YOU OUT

*

memory stitching
its gauze shroud
to fit any face

he will say to his friends
she was mean
he will have little interest
in diagramming sentences
the boy / has good taste
enormous capacities
for high-tech language
but will struggle
to bring his lunchbox home

I remember / you
you're / the one
I stared at in the / cloud

when I wasn't paying / attention
to people / on the ground

*

the three-year-old wore twenty dresses
to her preschool interview

her mother could not make her
change

take some off her mother pleaded
and the girl put on a second pair of tights

please I'm begging you
what will they think of us

the girl put all eight of her pastel barrettes
into her hair at once

she put on
her fuzzy green gloves

she would have worn four shoes but could not
get the second pair on top of the first pair

her mother cried you look like a mountain
who has come to live with me

she had trouble walking
from the car up to the school

trouble sitting
in the small chair that was offered

the headmistress said
my my   we are a stubborn personality

ACROSS THE BAY

If we throw our eyes way out to sea,
they thank us. All those corners
we've made them sit down in lately,
those objects with dust along
their seams.

Out here eyes find the edge
that isn't one.
Gray water, streak of pink,
little tap of sun,
and that storm off to the right
that seems to like us now.

How far can the wind carry
whatever lets go? Light
shining from dead stars
cradles our sleep. Secret light
no one reads by—
who owns that beam?
Who follows it far enough?

The month our son turned five
we drove between cotton fields
down to the bay. Thick layers
of cloud pouring into one another
as tractors furrowed the earth,
streams of gulls dipping down
behind. We talked about
the worms in their beaks.
How each thing on earth
searches out what it needs,
if it's lucky. And always
another question—*what if?*
what if?

Some day you'll go so far away
I'll die for missing you,
like millions of mothers
before me—how many friends
I suddenly have! Across the bay
a ship will be passing, tiny dot
between two ports meaning nothing
to me, carrying cargo useless to my life,
but I'll place my eyes on it
as if it held me up. Or you rode
that boat.

MY UNCLE'S FAVORITE COFFEE SHOP

Serum of steam rising from the cup,
what comfort to be known personally by *Barbara*,
her perfect pouring hand and starched ascot,
known as the two easy eggs and the single pancake,
without saying.
What pleasure for an immigrant—
anything without saying.

My uncle slid into his booth.
I cannot tell you—how I love this place.
He drained the water glass, noisily clinking his ice.
My uncle hailed from an iceless region.
He had definite ideas about water drinking.
I cannot tell you—all the time. But then he'd try.

My uncle wore a white shirt every day of his life.
He raised his hand against the roaring ocean
and the television full of lies.
He shook his head back and forth
from one country to the other
and his ticket grew longer.
Immigrants had double and nothing all at once.
Immigrants drove the taxis, sold the beer and Cokes.
When he found one note that rang true,
he sang it over and over inside.
Coffee, honey.
His eyes roamed the couples at other booths,
their loose banter and casual clothes.
But he never became them.

Uncle who finally left in a bravado moment
after 23 years, *to live in the old country forever,*
to stay and never come back,
maybe it would be peaceful now,
maybe for one minute,

I cannot tell you—how my heart has settled at last.
But he followed us to the sidewalk
saying, *Take care, Take care,*
as if he could not stand to leave us.

I cannot tell—

how we felt
to learn that the week he arrived,
he died. Or how it is now,
driving his parched streets,
feeling the booth beneath us as we order,
oh, anything, because if we don't,
nothing will come.

ENTHUSIASM IN TWO PARTS

Maybe a wasp will sting my throat again
so the high bouillon surge of joy
sweetens the day.
Shall I blink or wave?
Simply stand below the vine?
Since the stinger first pierced my throat
and a long-held note of gloom suddenly lifted,
I've considered poisons with surprise applications.
Happy venom.
Staring differently at bees, spiders,
centipedes, snakes.

*

We're more elastic than we thought.
Morning's pouf of goodwill
shrinks to afternoon's tight nod.
We deliver cake to aged ladies
who live alone,
just to keep some hope afloat.
Those who are known,
rightly or wrongly,
as optimists, have a heavier boat
than most. If we pause,
or simply look away,
they say, *What's wrong?*
They don't let us throw
anything overboard
even for a minute.
But that's the only way
we get it back.

OUR SON SWEARS HE HAS 102 GALLONS OF WATER IN HIS BODY

Somewhere a mistaken word distorts the sum:
divide becomes *multiply* so he'd wrestle his parents
who defy what he insists. *I did the problem*
and my teacher said I was right!
Light strokes the dashboard.
We are years away from its source.
Remember that jug of milk?
No way you're carrying one hundred of those!
But he knows. He always knows. We're idiots
without worksheets to back us up. His mother never remembers
what a megabyte means and his dad fainted on an airplane once
and smashed his head on the drinks cart. We're nice but we're
not always smart. It's the fact you live with, having parents.

Later in a calmer moment his dad recalculates
the sum and it comes out true.
Instead of carrying giant waterfalls inside,
we're streams, sweet pools, something to dip into
with an old metal cup, like the one we took camping,
that nobody could break.

MORNING GLORY

The faces of the teachers
know we have failed and failed
yet they focus beyond, on the windowsill
the names of distant galaxies
and trees.

We have come in dragging.
If someone would give us
a needle and thread, or send us
on a mission to collect something
at a store, we could walk for twenty years
sorting it out. How do we open,
when we are so full?

The teachers have more faith than we do.
They have organized into units.
We would appreciate units
if we gave them a chance.
Nothing will ever again be so clear.

The teachers look at our papers
when they would rather be looking at
a fine scallop of bark
or their fathers and mothers thin as lace,
their own teachers remaining in front
of a class at the back of their minds.
So many seasons of rain, sun, wind
have crystallized their teachers.
They shine like something on a beach.
But we don't see that yet.

We're fat with binders and forgetting.
We're shaping the name of a new love
on the underside of our thumb.
We're diagnosing rumor and trouble

and fear. We hear the teachers
as if they were far off, speaking
down a tube. Sometimes
a whole sentence gets through.

But the teachers don't give up.
They rise, dress, appear before us
crisp and hopeful. They have a plan.
If cranes can fly 1,000 miles
or that hummingbird return from Mexico
to find, curled on its crooked fence, a new vine,
surely. We may dip into the sweet
together, if we hover long enough.

BOY AND EGG

Every few minutes, he wants
to march the trail of flattened rye grass
back to the house of muttering
hens. He too could make
a bed in hay. Yesterday the egg so fresh
it felt hot in his hand and he pressed it
to his ear while the other children
laughed and ran with a ball, leaving him,
so little yet, too forgetful in games,
ready to cry if the ball brushed him,
riveted to the secret of birds
caught up inside his fist,
not ready to give it over
to the refrigerator
or the rest of the day.

THE TIME

Summer is the time to write. I tell myself this
in winter especially. Summer comes,
I want to tumble with the river
over rocks and mossy dams.

A fish drifting upside down.
Slow accordions sweeten the breeze.

The Sanitary Mattress Factory says,
"Sleep Is Life."
Why do I think of forty ways to spend an afternoon?

Yesterday someone said, "It gets late so early."
I wrote it down. I was going to do something with it.
Maybe it is a title and this life is the poem.

LAST SONG FOR THE MEND-IT SHOP

1.

Today some buildings were blown up,
rounded shoulders, the shoulders
of women no one has touched for a long time.

Men and women watched from their offices
then went back to filing papers.
A drinking fountain hummed.

I translate this from the deep love
I feel for old buildings.
I translate this from my scream.

2.

The rosebushes held on so tightly
we could not get them out.
Under the sign that promised
to stitch things together,
the thorny weathered MEND-IT
fading fast now
fading hard,

Jim heaved his shovel.
We were loosening dirt
around the heavy central roots,
trespassing, trying to save
at least the roses
before bulldozers came,
before the land was shaved
and the Mexican men and women
who tend with such a gracious bending
disappeared. They were already gone

and their roses would not let go.
We bit hard on the sweetness,
snipping, in all our names,
the last lavish orange heads,
our teeth pressed tightly together.

3.

This looks like a good place
to build something ugly.
Let's do it. A snack
shop. Let's erase
the board. Who can build
faster? You could fit
a hundred cars here.
It's only a house
some guy lived in
ninety years. And it's so
convenient to downtown.
That old theater nobody goes to
anymore, who cares if it's
the last theater like that
in the United States?
Knock it out so we can build
a bank that goes bankrupt
in two years. Don't hang
on.

4.

Some days I can't lift
the glint of worry.
We go around together.
Soon we will wear
each other's names.

Already we bathe
in the river of lost shoes.
I fall into photographs.
Someone lives inside
those windows.

Before they demolish
the Honolulu bakery,
women in hair nets
and white dresses
lock arms on the counter.
Someone buys
their last world-famous
golden lemon cake.

Take a card, any card.
The magic dissolving recipe
for buildings with frills?
We will not know what
it tasted like.

HOW FAR IS IT TO THE LAND WE LEFT?

On the first day of his life
the baby opens his eyes
and gets tired doing even that.
He cries when they place a cap on his head.
Too much, too much!

Later the whole world will touch him
and he won't even flinch.

OUR PRINCIPAL

beat his wife.
We did not know it then.
We knew his slanted-stripe
ties.
We said, "Good morning"
in our cleanest voices.
He stood beside the door
of the office
where all our unborn
report cards lived.
He had twins
and reddish hair.
Later the news
would seep
along the gutters,
chilly stream
of autumn rain.
My mother,
newspaper dropped down
on the couch, staring
out the window—
All those years I told you
pay good attention to
what he says.

POINT OF ROCKS, TEXAS

The stones in my heart
do not recognize your name.
Lizard poking his nose from a crack
considers us both strangers.

This wide terrain,
like a gray-green bottom of an ocean,
gives no sign.

If we have been here since whatever blow it was
toppled these boulders,
if we are brief as lightning in the arrow-shaped
wisp of cloud—
on top of this peak, there are no years.
A single mound rises off the plain.

There I would make my house, you say, pointing.
And I want to take the hand that points
and build with it. Place it against my eyes,
lips, heart, make a roof.
If each day, history were a new sentence—
but then what would happen to
the rocks, the trees?

From this distance every storm
looks like a simple stripe.

PAUSE

The boy needed
to stop by the road.
What pleasure to let
the engine quit droning
inside the long heat,
to feel where they were.
Sometimes
she was struck by this
as if a plank had slapped
the back of her head.

They were thirsty
as grasses
leaning sideways
in the ditch,
Big Bluestem
and Little Barley,
Texas Cupgrass,
Hairy Crabgrass,
Green Sprangletop.
She could stop at a store
selling only grass names
and be happy.

They would pause
and the pause
seep into them,
fence post,
twisted wire,
brick chimney
without its house,
pollen taking flight
toward the cities.

Something would gather
back into place.
Take the word "home"
for example,
often considered
to have an address.
How it could sweep across you
miles beyond the last
neat packages of ice
and nothing be wider
than its pulse.
Out here,
everywhere,
the boy looking away from her
across the fields.

LUGGAGE

she carries her eyes from country to country
in Rome adding the crisp slant of sky
as earlier she gathered crowds of coffee cups
frothing hot miles   a scared man with a name tag
planted firmly on one shoulder
rows of empty chairs   buckled cases
and the bags from India tied and tied with rope

as she gets older the luggage grows
lighter and heavier   together
strange how the soil absorbs water
and is quickly dry again
how the filled room points to the window

haggard smiles of waiting strangers
brief flash and falling back to separateness
how much everyone is carrying
moving belt   the artifacts expand
now a basket of apricots
a mini-stove from England

an Italian grandfather weeps on the shoulder
of his glorious departing girl
the woman takes it in   thinking
how this world has everything and offers it
how it is good we only have two hands

THE TURTLE SHRINE NEAR CHITTAGONG

Humps of shell emerge from dark water.
Believers toss hunks of bread,
hoping the fat reptilian heads
will loom forth from the murk
and eat. Meaning: *you have been
heard.*

I stood, breathing the stench of mud
and rotten dough, and could not feel
encouraged. Climbed the pilgrim hill
where prayers in tissue radiant tubes
were looped to a tree. Caught in
their light, a hope washed over me
small as the hope of stumbling feet
but did not hold long enough
to get me down.

Rickshas crowded the field,
announced by tinny bells.
The friend beside me, whose bread
floated and bobbed,
grew grim. They're full, I told him.
But they always eat mine.

That night I told the man I love most
he came from hell. It was also
his birthday. We gulped lobster
over a white tablecloth in a country
where waves erase whole villages, annually,
and don't even make our front page.
Waiters forded the lulling currents
of heat. Later, my mosquito net
had holes.

All night, I was pitching something,
crumbs or crusts, into that bottomless pool
where the spaces between our worlds take root.
He would forgive me tomorrow.
But I wanted a mouth to rise up
from the dark, a hand,
any declarable body part, to swallow
or say, *This is water, that is land.*

KEEP DRIVING

Atsuko
steering her smooth burgundy car
past orange cranes
and complicated shipyards
has always lived in Yokohama,
but possibly this neighborhood
sprang up over the weekend
when we were off beside the sea.
Massive concrete, tones of gray.
Every day something changes in a city.
A woman pulls groceries home
in a metallic cart past five thousand
beige apartments,
but she will find her own
and twist the key.
We respect her.
Iron girders for a new
construction.
Rafters. Pipes.
Legions of coordinated
stoplights.
Atsuko cannot see any street
she recognizes,
one roadside tree
staked to bamboo
looks vaguely familiar.
She has seen other trees like that.
Will I keep my eyes open please?
Let her know if I spot any clues?
*Remember who
you are talking to*, I say,
and we both laugh very loudly,
which is not something
I thought I would get to do
in Japan this soon.

We veer under highways,
elevated tracks, clouds.
The red train zips by smoothly overhead,
but all our streets go one way the wrong way
and I'm still confused by her steering wheel
on the right side, my foot punching
an invisible clutch.
What has she done?
Atsuko keeps apologizing
as we circle shoe shops dress shops party shops—
obviously her city is bigger
than she thought it was.
We must get gas.
Another day Mount Fuji-san looming
on the horizon
might help us gain our bearings,
but it's invisible today.
Right now
everything is gray.
Only the red train for punctuation.
She has never been more lost.
Keep driving, I whisper,
Kyoto, Hokkaido,
villages, rice fields,
how can I be lost or found
if I have never been here before?
Your hotel is hiding, she groans.
Instead we find the Toyota dock
for the third time
in three hours.
Tricky city clicking its rhythms
into each U-turn, crosswalk,
the intricate red blood
networks of people,
into the secret hidden dirt.

Soon I will feel as grounded
as the citizens of the foreign cemetery
on the one high hill
who came here planning to
leave.

THE DIFFICULT LIFE OF A YOKOHAMA LEAF

Each train that passes
whips a gust of wind
a heavy heat.

Each car,
each choke of pavement,
every new building
with two hundred windows,
every metal edge.

They don't say "smog" here,
they say, "It's a cloudy day."

The leaf is supposed to remember
what a leaf does:
green code of leaf language,
shapely grace & frill.

Beyond the city
green hills shimmer & float.
They disappear
in the steamy heat.

But they give courage to the single leaf
on the tightly propped branch
by the Delightful Discovery Drugstore.

LISTENING TO POETRY IN A LANGUAGE I DO NOT UNDERSTAND

Picture a blue door,
a shiny pipe the rain runs through.
Yellow flower
with twenty supple lips.

I like how you move your hands.
The black T-shirt you have worn
for the last three days
drapes over baggy blue pants.
You stop so abruptly,
I fall into the breath
of the person next to me.

We may look at this poem
from the mountain above the roof
or stand under it
where it casts a cool shadow.

Is this your family home?
Your grandfather's tiny Buddha?

One word rolls across the floor,
lodging under the slipper
of the man who has felt uncomfortable
all day.

Now he knows what to say.

∞

FROM THIS DISTANCE

He would take a small folded paper from his pocket—
"I have been diagnosed with schizophrenia"—
the same moment you wanted to kiss him.

What was he wringing in his hands all those years?
The chicken refused to smoke a cigarette.
Seven white stones circled a thistle.
You would have gone with him,
but he climbed a high fence.

There was always this Y in the road.
Red checkered jacket draped
over picnic table.
Arrangement of broken bottles
in the doorway of the Paris Hatters.

He would take a word and remove its shirt.
The open heart of the o, the wink of an e,
the long trapped mystery of the crossed t;
and the squirrel gathering what it needed,
scrambling high into the branches,
dropping shells on his face
as he stood under the tree looking up.

SAD MAIL

It's strange to think how letters used to be letters, letting you know someone liked you, saying pleasant dull things like, *How are you, we are fine*, making you wish for more but not weighing you, really. Now the letters are funnels of want, requests for favors, Please do what you can, Help me get into Yaddo (where I have never been), Tell my teachers I am a good student, Don't you think I would be excellent in that program overseas? I want to send everyone overseas. I want to be there myself, where my mail can't find me. It's startling to miss the sweet dim-witted reports of summers & boyfriends, journeys & pets, the scented lilac envelopes. Now the envelopes are long & white, letters begin *How long it has been since we really connected* & pole-vault into the request by the second paragraph. And no one ever says you have months to do this in. You have till tomorrow. I am lonely with my mail. Yesterday I went out walking before the mailman came, & the street was filled with carcasses of empty envelopes, dampened & tattered, the wings of exotic insects lost without their bodies. I wanted to bend & reclaim them, smooth them, fill them with unsigned notes, & drop them into my neighbor's shining boxes. One at a time.

PUBLIC OPINION

What they say first, what they say next.

I never saw a public walking around anyway.

They throw it up in the air like a ball.

No one has her hands out.

If it hits you in the head, it hurts.

Bouncing, it dissolves.

I'm not worried about it.

Give me your pants,
and I'll hem them.

How long do you want them?

OPEN HOUSE

I work as hard as I can
to have nothing to do.

Birds climb their rich ladder
of choruses.

They have tasted the top of the tree,
but they are not staying.

The whole sky says,
Your move.

QUIET OF THE MIND

A giant, puffed, and creamy cloud
ignited on the right-hand horizon
from Presidio to Marfa as the western sky
dropped solidly into deepest blue.
We who were driving north on that road
pulled the car over, pulled it over
because the grasses in their lanky goldenness
called for standing alongside them
while the whole sky
held.

Inside that lit stillness,
we drank the swelling breath that would
unfold on its own for months
whenever the cities pressed us,
rubbed us down, or called out
people, people, people.

RETURN

Build my home here
on the spot of old time.
I'm sure I have failed you
one thousand ways,
you ancient clock,
you stockpot of moments.

Look how the first thing I do
upon entering the house
is remove my watch.

It's in your honor.

VOCABULARY OF DEARNESS

How a single word
may shimmer and rise
off the page, a wafer of
syllabic light, a bulb
of glowing meaning,
whatever the word,
try "tempestuous" or "suffer,"
any word you have held
or traded so it lives a new life
the size of two worlds.
Say you carried it
up a hill and it helped you
move. Without this
the days would be thin sticks
thrown down in a clutter of leaves,
and where is the rake?

POLLEN

When weeds eat the playhouse
what does that say about the family?

The ball left at the base of the tree
loses its breath shrinking into

a stump or clump of dirt and the mole comes
and the earth drums up into little mounds

nobody kicks. Then what year is it?
Maybe the door to the big house opens and a man comes out.

A woman comes out drying her hands.
Dinner is almost ready but there's no one else

to eat it. Besides the man and the woman.
Maybe only the woman.

Or there's no dinner.
The door to the playhouse stuck open not swinging

and light comes through
replete with pollen of cedar and foxglove

and something else is going to be planted
in the ditch by the road

on the bank of the river but there will not be
a child to tell its story. How will that change the story?

If the fox puts on her lavender gloves just as you shut your eyes.
If in the night something touches your sleeping cheek

and startles you and it is the fox
but you forget to offer her tea in the playhouse

then what year would you be sipping?
What would that say about the person you became?

THE LAST DAY OF AUGUST

A man in a lawn chair
with a book on his lap

realizes pears are falling
from the tree right beside him.

Each makes a round,
full sound in the grass.

Perhaps the stem takes an hour
to loosen and let go.

This man who has recently written words
to his father forty years in the birthing:

I was always afraid of you.
When would you explode next?

has sudden reverence for the pears.
If a dark bruise rises,

if ants inhabit the juicy crack,
or the body remains firm, unscarred,

remains secret till tomorrow...
By then the letter to his father

may be lying open on a table.
We gather pears in baskets, sacks.

What will we do with everything
that has been given us? Ginger pears, pear pies,

fingers weighing flesh.
Which will be perfect under the skin?

It is hard not to love the pile of peelings
growing on the counter next to the knife.

I STILL HAVE EVERYTHING YOU GAVE ME

It is dusty on the edges.

Slightly rotten.

I guard it without thinking.

Focus on it once a year
when I shake it out in the wind.

I do not ache.

I would not trade.

∞

ACKNOWLEDGMENTS

Thanks to the editors of the following journals where some of these poems first appeared:

Alaska Quarterly Review, Atlanta Review, The Atlantic Monthly, Cat's Ear, Chaminade Literary Review, Chili Verde Review, Clackamas Literary Review, Fine Madness, Five Points, Grafitti Rag, Green Mountains Review, Hawai'i Review, Hayden's Ferry Review, Herman Review, Hurakan, Indiana Review, The Kenyon Review, Many Mountains Moving, The New York Times, One Trick Pony, Paragraph, Poetry Kanto (Japan), Rain City Review, Rio Grande Review, Solo, Tampa Review, ¡TEX!, Two Rivers Review.

Individual poems appeared in the following books:

"Elevator" appeared in *I Feel a Little Jumpy Around You*, edited by Naomi Shihab Nye and Paul B. Janeczko (Simon & Schuster, 1996);

"The Small Vases from Hebron" appeared in *The Best American Poetry 1996*, edited by Adrienne Rich (Scribner, 1996);

"Darling " appeared in *Contemporary American Poetry*, Sixth Edition, edited by A. Poulin, Jr. (Houghton Mifflin, 1996);

"Always Bring a Pencil" appeared in *Minutes of the Lead Pencil Club*, edited by Bill Henderson (Pushcart Press, 1996);

"The Rider" appeared in *The Place My Words Are Looking For*, edited by Paul B. Janeczko (Bradbury Press, 1990);

"My Uncle's Favorite Coffee Shop" appeared in *Written with a Spoon: A Poet's Cookbook*, edited by Nancy Fay and Judith Rafaela Sherman (Asher Publishing, New Mexico, 1995);

"Last Song for the Mend-It Shop" appeared in *Travel Alarm* (a chapbook), (Wings Press, Houston, 1993);

"The Time" appeared in *Invisible*, a chapbook, (Trilobite Press, Denton, 1989).

*

Deep thanks to the John Simon Guggenheim Memorial Foundation for their heartening support.

Also I am grateful to Madison, without whom it would be Ticonderoga #1 pencils all the way.

"Listening to Poetry in a Language I Do Not Understand" is for Shuntarō Tanikawa.

"How Far is it to the Land We Left?" is for Aidan Artemus Gurovitsch.

"String" is for Phyllis Theroux.

"F" by Denise Levertov, from *Poems 1968-1972*. Copyright © 1970 by Denise Levertov. Reprinted by permission of New Directions Publishing Corp.

∞

ABOUT THE AUTHOR

Naomi Shihab Nye lives in San Antonio, Texas. Her recent books include *Habibi* (a novel for teens), *Lullaby Raft* (a picture book) and *Never in a Hurry* (essays). Her books of poems are *Red Suitcase* (BOA) and *Words under the Words: Selected Poems*. She has edited four prize-winning anthologies of poetry for young readers and is a Guggenheim Fellow for 1997–1998.

BOA EDITIONS, LTD.: AMERICAN POETS CONTINUUM SERIES

∞